I wish to acknowledge
all those beautiful beings
who have shared their losses,
tears and sorrows with me

for David

Publisher's ISBN: 0-9609888-2-3

Printed in the United States of America

Published by Red Rose Press.
P.O. Box 24, Encino, California 91426
First Edition, 1986

Second Printing 1986

TO HEAL AGAIN

towards serenity
and the resolution
of grief

by
Rusty Berkus

with illustrations by
Christa Wollan

Red Rose Press
Encino, California
1986

The quiet "little deaths"
of everyday existence
are mourned as much as those
of resounding magnitude,
for grief makes no comparisons
nor judgments,
and has no understanding
of degree

Rusty Berkus

You sit in the shadow of sorrow
seeking, searching
for the magic that will make the pain
go away

Weep what you must weep,
not only for this loss,
but for all other losses
you have sustained
in this life

Surrender into the memory
of what once was,
and can no longer be

This Winter of your life
will pass,
as all seasons do

Stay in your season
of Winterness
as long as need be,
for everything you feel
is appropriate

There is no right way
to grieve —
there is just Your way

It will take
as long as it takes

It is important
to be ever so gentle,
kind, loving and giving
to yourself right now

and
to let others
be ever so gentle,
kind, loving and giving to you

Remember how deserving
you are
of gentleness, kindness
lovingness and givingness

No one ever said it was easy
to let go, let be, let life do
what it is supposed to do

Perhaps you feel
you are the only one
in the universe

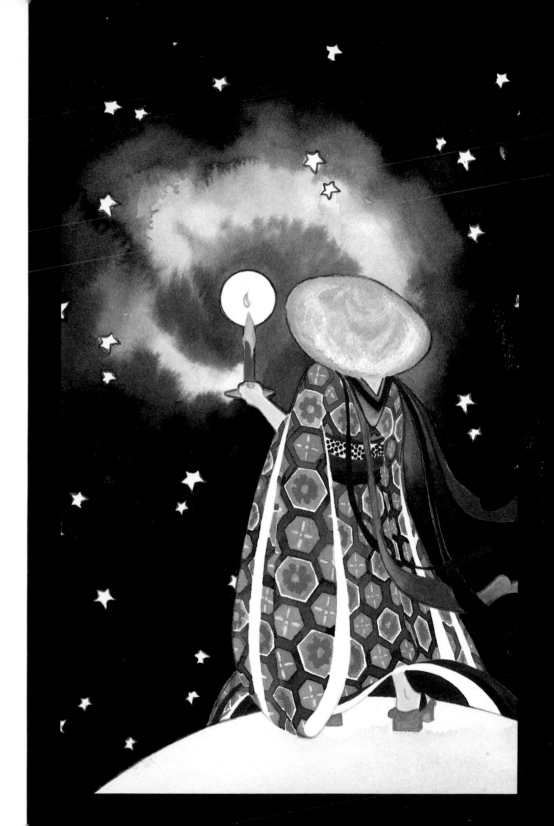

but out of your loss
is an interconnectedness
with all humanity —
for you are One with everyone
who has ever mourned

When you live fully,
your vulnerability takes you
through the shadows of Winter
where you feel you may never
see the sun again

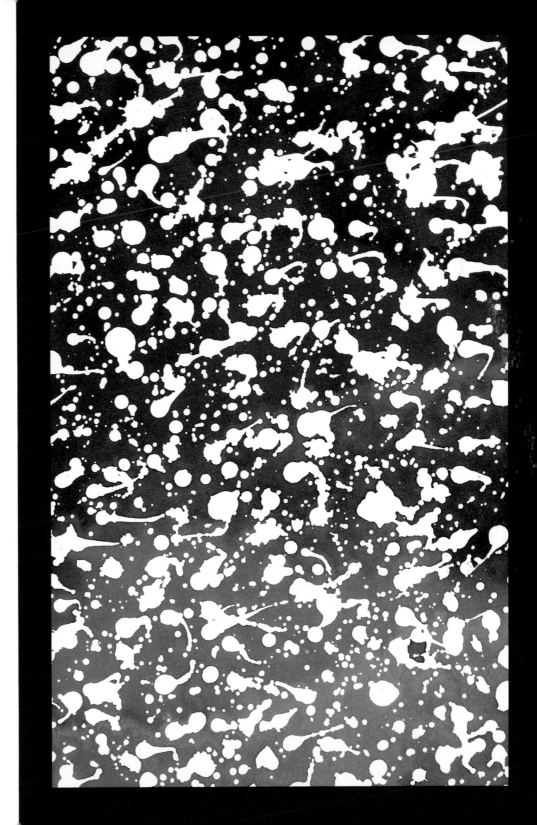

To cease living fully
because you fear the Winter shadow
is never to see the sun at all

Judge not
the appearance
of this loss

Behind the darkest cloud
of the dreary Winter chill
is a Springtime
begging to burst forth

Bless this pain
for it will bear its perfect gift
to you in its perfect time

Out of your yearning
for comfort, calm,
growth and belief,
out of an aching void,
comes a divine mystical force

*It longs to thaw
the frozen Winter
of your grief*

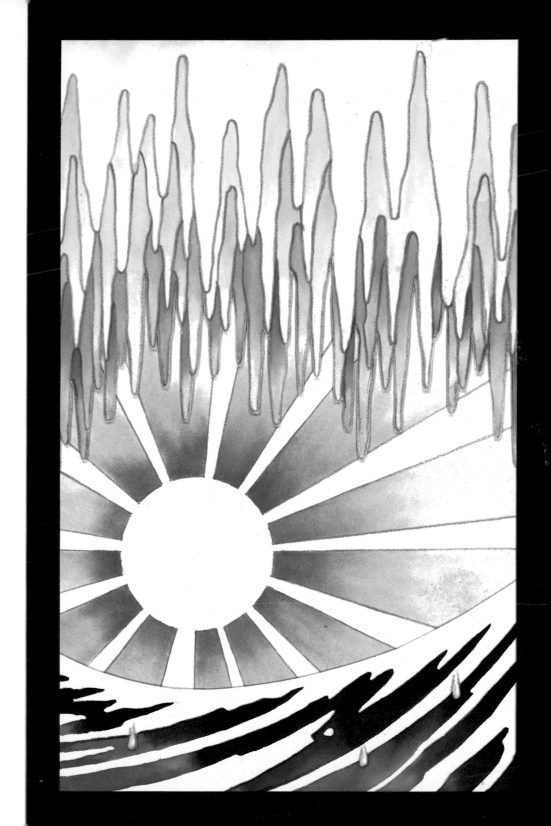

for the invisible world of Spirit
will be your greatest power
with which to heal

Know beyond all knowing
that through the power
of the Spirit within
you will befriend
your highest Self

The exquisiteness of this Friendship
leads you to realms of compassion,
humility and service —
to a fulfillment
you never knew existed

into a holy instant of Springtime —
of harmony, creativity,
and the opportunity to once again
master your life.

Behold,
you will sit in the radiant sun
without sorrow
no longer seeking, searching
for the magic
that will make the pain
go away —
ready to love,
to smile, to sing,
to give,
to heal again

and you will have stopped asking
why

About the Author

Rusty Berkus is a poet, composer, lyricist and has received her Masters degree in Marriage and Family Counseling.
Through her own personal loss and in counseling countless others in their grief process, Rusty has discovered that each of us needs to grant ourselves permission to grieve, and that there is always a way out of the dark night of the soul. "By surrendering into our pain and trusting the Spirit within to do the work, we open ourselves to the miracle of healing."

About the Artist

Christa Wollan is a graphic artist and illustrator presently working with Kissler Company, Inc., a design studio in Beverly Hills, California.
Recognizing the tremendous need in the world for visual imagery that heals and uplifts, Christa devotes her work to serving that need. "In many ways, life and art are one and the same. Just as a painting has its balance of dark and light, the enormous canvas of the universe maintains its own perfect balance. In its time, darkness is always followed by light. Trust and know that God loves you always."